# QUALITY OF SERVICE
## Measuring Performance
## for Voluntary Organisations

# QUALITY OF SERVICE

## Measuring Performance
## for Voluntary Organisations

**by Alan Lawrie**

**A joint NCVO/Directory of Social Change Contract Culture publication**

# QUALITY OF SERVICE

By **Alan Lawrie**

Cover design by Nicholas Karides

First published by the Directory of Social Change with the
National Council for Voluntary Organisations, with financial
assistance from the Allied Dunbar Charitable Trust

ISBN 0-907164-82-X

Printed in Britain by Biddles of Guildford


**Directory of Social Change**, Radius Works, Back Lane,
London NW3 1HL   Tel. 071-284 4364

**National Council for Voluntary Organisations,**
 26 Bedford Square, London WC1B 3HU
Tel. 071-636 4066

# CONTENTS

1. Introduction                          5

2. Some basic terms and ideas            8

3. Performance measurement               16

4. Value for money                       42

5. A question of quality                 52

6. Managing the new relationship         77

7. Management implications               88

Bibliography                             92

# Chapter 1
# INTRODUCTION

Voluntary organisations exist in turbulent times. Demands for their services continues to increase, but, obtaining adequate funding to pay for their services is increasingly difficult.

The voluntary sector (a term still used to describe small community groups and also large million pound operations) is now seen as a "partner" working to provide services alongside statutory bodies.

Voluntary organisations are having to work out, very quickly, how to respond to a number of new issues, sometimes optimistically called "challenges":

The issues include:

● A growing demand from funding bodies that voluntary groups prove that they are managing their income in an effective way and that they are providing "value for money".

● The development of a "contract culture". Grants are increasingly being replaced by contracts for specific services. Contracts, (often called, service agreements) involve a much more systematic and defined relationship between the purchaser of the contract (eg the local authority) and the contractor (the voluntary group).

● The use of a new "management language". Terms such as "performance indicators", "occupancy levels" and "inputs and outputs" are being used more and more. To continue to provide an effective service voluntary organisations need to understand this language and work within it.

- The central commitment contained in recent government initiatives in the field of community care and housing, to create "comparisons" between service providers, so that people can choose within a "marketplace".

- An increased commitment to the issue of "quality" – that the user of a service has the right to expect services to perform to standard.

In short, voluntary organisations need to come to terms with some new concepts and techniques so that they can continually prove that they use public money for the purposes for which it was intended in an effective and efficient way.

This may not be all that difficult. Many voluntary organisations have always operated "on a shoestring", at costs considerably cheaper than other providers.

However, many of the management concepts and measurement techniques described in this book were designed for a commercial or industrial purpose. They are only now being imported into the social care and community development arenas.

This book is intended to help voluntary organisations to unravel these concepts and techniques, identify those that are genuinely useful and enable voluntary organisations to negotiate effectively with funding bodies.

# The structure of the book

*Chapter two* looks at some basic definitions and concepts relevant to this subject. A simple model of how organisations can be measured is explained and discussed.

*Chapter three* reviews the issue of performance measurement. Guidance is given on the use and abuse of performance indicators and a range of possible indicators is outlined.

*Chapter four* focuses on the issue of "Value For Money" studies. It looks at what should be included in a value for money study. It also describes the problems involved in trying to use a Value for Money approach to make comparisons between organisations.

*Chapter five* introduces the issue of Quality and Quality Assurance. The different dimensions of quality are considered and practical advice is given on drawing up a quality assurance system.

*Chapter six* emphasises the changing relations between voluntary organisations and their funding body. It suggest how the relationship could develop and outlines how monitoring arrangements could work.

*Chapter seven* poses questions about the managerial and organisational implications of using performance measurement systems. How can they change the management process of the organisation? What value does it bring to an organisation?.

*Chapter eight* concludes with a bibliography of useful follow up reading.

Chapter 2

# SOME BASIC IDEAS AND TERMS

## Inputs, outputs and outcomes

A standard model for measuring performance is one based around identifying and monitoring inputs, outputs and outcomes. Over the past ten years this model has been used extensively in the public sector.

### Inputs

Inputs are:

- **Money**
  (donations, grants and contract fees)
- **Resources**
  (equipment, facilities and buildings).
- **People's time**
  (staff, volunteers, committee members etc).

Ideas, energy and innovation, one could argue, are also inputs, but are harder to record.

### Process

The process is what the organisation chooses to do with the inputs (eg. what it spends its money on, how it manages its staff) in order to create outputs.

Box 2.1

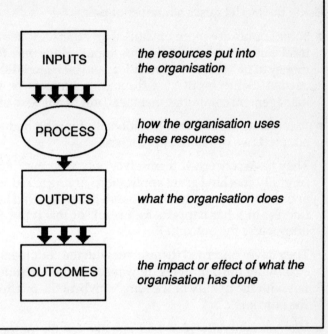

## Analysing what an organisation does

Every organisation can be described in the following way:

INPUTS — *the resources put into the organisation*

PROCESS — *how the organisation uses these resources*

OUTPUTS — *what the organisation does*

OUTCOMES — *the impact or effect of what the organisation has done*

## Outputs

Outputs are:

- **Services**
  (a counselling service, a drop in centre)
- **Products**
  (a training pack, a piece of computer software)
- **Activities**
  (a community festival)

that the organisation carries out in order to meet its objectives based on what it sees as the needs of its users.

9

# Outcomes

The outcome is the impact, both the short term and long term, created by the output.

The case study on page 12 shows how this model could be used for a community worker.

Using the model raises a number of points:

● Some inputs are more obvious than others. Money from a local authority is one obvious input. However, for that money to produce an output, ideas and managerial skills are needed. Some inputs (eg through volunteers or unpaid management committee members) might not be so obvious.

● It could be argued that traditionally funding bodies have adopted two different approaches:

They have concerned themselves only with the "input" by carefully checking grant applications, trying to reduce costs and once the money has been handed over showed little real interest in what happens as a result of this input (i.e. the output and the outcome).

They have concerned themselves with the "numbers game" – counting the output (eg. how many people attended) and not with the quality of the long term benefits or effects (i.e. the outcome).

● We can generally plan and manage for the outputs of a service or activity. The outcomes are much harder to plan, predict and therefore measure.

For example, a training centre decides to use its resources to put on a course for unemployed people who are interested in careers in computers.

The outputs are relatively easy to define; twelve unemployed people registered for the course and at the end of it seven of them were given a certificate to show that they had completed sixteen hours of basic computer training.

The outcomes are much more harder to accurately measure. One positive outcome might be that two students went onto a more extensive course at the local college and that another got a job as a result of the course. However, some of the other students might well have had a positive outcome or longer term benefit. One student may have decided that she is not interested in computers after all, but feels much more positive about herself as a result of attending the course. Still a positive outcome, but much harder to predict, monitor and record.

Outcomes are sometimes difficult to prove as it can be difficult to establish that an output was directly responsible for a particular outcome.

How can a drugs agency that has made education work with young people a high priority objectively prove that its campaign work was the output that led to a change in behaviour amongst young people? Outcomes usually take a longer time to develop – the output might have ended (eg the project has been wound up or moved onto other objectives) without any knowledge of the outcome. It could be that the outcome is a "side effect" of the work.

Despite these difficulties, outcomes are very important. They are, in essence, what was actually achieved (as opposed to what was produced). It is important that people involved in funding and managing voluntary organisations emphasise that, at the end of the day, it is the quality and effectiveness of outcome that matters and not only the cost of the input or the quantity of the output.

Box 2.2

# Inputs, outputs and outcomes

Newton Neighbourhood Association secured funding to employ a community worker on their estate. The worker produced a work programme for the first six months that had three main aims:

• To support the creation of tenants associations.
• To provide practical help and advice to local people.
• To identify local needs and carry out a fund raising campaign for the neighbourhood association.

The project's inputs, outputs and outcomes were:

**Inputs:**

• The salary of the community worker.
• The grant for the workers running costs.
• Free office accommodation in the local estate hall.

Other inputs were less obvious:

• Volunteer time and effort.
• Support and help from local voluntary organisations.

**Outputs:**

• 140 hours work with local people on setting up a tenants association.
• 24 Advice sessions attended by 88 local people.
• Production of a report on the needs of the community.
• 35 hours of work with local parents on a campaign for a school crossing.
• A fundraising campaign contacting over 150 potential supporters.

**Outcomes:**

The outcomes are harder to objectively record. However looking back at the work, three months later, it was possible to point to the following outcomes:

• The tenants association had elected a committee that was now strong enough to meet without the constant support of the community worker.
• 42 of the people who attended the advice session had some sort of a positive result.
• The report on local needs had been positively received by the Council. There was hope of more permanent funding.

# Measuring organisations

Broadly speaking there are three ways to look at effectiveness:

## 1. A performance model

Collecting information (usually through a system of performance indicators) to judge what the organisation does over time. Performance measurement checks that the organisation is making effective progress towards completing its stated plans or objectives.

## 2. A comparative model

Comparing the costs and performance to similar organisations or to possible alternative ways of delivering the same service. Making comparisons is an essential aspect of a "Value For Money" framework.

## 3. Through a Quality Assurance system

The identification of what the users of a service regard as important about how the service works. These issues are then developed into quality standards. Systems and processes are then monitored to ensure that the agreed standards are always met.

## Summary

1. How easy is it to identify the inputs, outputs and outcomes of the services your organisation provides?

2. How do they relate to what you intend to do?

3. Measuring performance invariably raises questions about what short and long term goals you hope to achieve and what values underpin your work. How clear are they? How much clarity is there between workers, volunteers, committee members about the purpose of the organisation and the methods and processes it should use?

4. Putting aside the interests and requirements of funders, how well do you evaluate your work?

Box 2.3

# A note about evaluation

There is a history within the voluntary sector of evaluation, a process of objectively reviewing how an organisation works to see if it meets its original aims and values.

Evaluation is an important part of good management and organisational practice particularly when it is a regular planned activity.

This book looks mainly at how to develop systems and techniques so that a voluntary organisation can prove its value to a funding body. Although, similar techniques (and terminology) are sometimes used, proving why an organisation should continue to exist is a narrower process than evaluation in the true sense of the word.

In the bibliography, a number of useful books of evaluation are listed.

*Throughout the book, the points made in each chapter are illustrated through a case study at the end of the chapter. This shows how the Hill Street Community Centre responds to the issues and ideas presented in the chapter.*

## Hill Street Community Centre
### >> *the continuing story*

Hilary, the new co-ordinator at Hill Street Community Centre, first encountered the "new management language" at a conference of local voluntary groups. Speaker after speaker referred to "indicators", "quality" and "outcomes" as a basis of a new partnership between the public and voluntary sectors. It seemed as though each speaker had at least three new words which they took pleasure in using.

Hilary felt puzzled. The centre provided activities that local people demanded and to a greater or lesser extent had a say in running. It did so with very little money. This new language did not seem to fit in with the practical day to day experience of running a community service.

For example, the centre's two minibuses worked night and day, driven by volunteers, and carrying a scarcely imaginable variety of passengers from just about every club or group in the area – when not doing their regular daily pick-up rounds of children for the after-school English Language class and for old people to get to their lunch clubs. What were the outcomes here?

Looking round the room, Hilary realised that other people looked puzzled and as the speakers went onto talk about "quality standards", "value for money" and "performance targets" they looked even more confused, but, of course no one ever stopped to ask what did it all mean. It reminded Hilary of the children's story, "The Emperor's New Clothes" in which no-one would point out that the Emperor had been "taken for a ride" for fear of being called stupid.

**Chapter 3**

# PERFORMANCE MEASUREMENT

## Performance measurement systems

A great deal of effort has been focused on establishing performance measurement systems for public sector organisations. As the voluntary sector is increasingly recognised as an important service provider (rather than a "fringe" or provider of "extras"), it is hardly surprising that attempts have been made to apply the same measurement to voluntary organisations as has been developed throughout the public sector.

Performance measurement systems are seen as having the following benefits:

- They provide data by which an organisation can be judged to see if it is working in the way that it said it would and is consistently delivering the intended quantity and quality of service.

- They can tell people what they should be able to expect (e.g. repairs should be carried out within three days). Funders, staff and users fully understand what kind of service is to be expected and are able, therefore, to identify failings.

- They provide a focus for managers. A performance measurement system can alert managers to problems or weaknesses and enable them to take action to ensure effective performance. Advocates of performance measurement systems would argue that "if you are not able to measure what is happening – than how can you manage it?".

- They can provide the basis for making comparisons between organisations carrying out the same task.

- They can give an organisation a sense of purpose and enable staff to recognise achievements over a set time.

Many government bodies have enthusiastically launched into performance measurement systems without given much thought to what precise information they actually need to collect. Often the cost of collecting the information is ignored. It is sometimes difficult to establish what exactly the collected information is used for and what impact it has on future plans or decisions.

Frequently, performance measurement systems degenerate into a "number crunching" exercise – a routine chore whereby arbitrarily chosen sets of numbers are collected together and are passed onto a monitoring officer. They rarely reflect the actual work of the organisation. There is a very real danger of developing performance measurement systems that record only what is easy to record rather than what is important.

There is a further problem of language. The terminology used in performance measurement is often mechanistic, perhaps more suited to accountancy or to a manufacturing enterprise. In fact, one of the first real attempt to develop performance measurement systems was in the Soviet Union in the development of central planning within the command economy – with disastrous results.

Many organisations have found the concepts of performance measurement difficult to apply to a field as complex and sometimes intangible as, for example, running an elderly day centre. Often this "difficulty" means that performance measurement systems focus on the quantity of the service (eg. how many people used it) rather than the quality and long term effectiveness of the service users received.

Nor is there agreement about what the language of performance measurement actually means. Funding organisations, particularly central government departments, use the terminology in a very loose way causing confusion and disarray. The box below attempts to provide some working definitions of the main terms used, based on their more frequent use.

Box 3.1

---

# Definitions

**Performance**
What happens and what is done over a fixed timescale.

**Performance Indicator**
A specific measure used in a planned way to record an aspect of performance.
*Example:*
In Longstreet Housing Association the number of emergency repairs reported within a month is one indicator. The average time taken to respond to them is a separate indicator.

**Performance Expectations or Performance Standards**
An agreed minimum level of performance that users should always be able to expect.
*Example:*
A clear commitment that all emergency repairs will always be attended to within eight hours of being reported to the office. The Association will organise itself so that it should always be able to meet this standard. It then monitors itself to ensure that, in practice, it is able to meet its commitment.

**Performance Target**
A commitment to increase the standard of performance within a set time
*Example:*
An association states that by the end of the year it intends to improve its services so that all notification of emergency repairs will be responded to within six hours rather than the current standard time of eight hours.

---

# Collecting performance management information

Most performance measurement systems are based on different sets of indicators. Broadly speaking there are four types of indicators in common use:

## 1. Cost indicators

Cost indicators are used to measure the financial performance of the service being provided and to collect data on the cost, income received, or profit/loss in a given period.

## 2. Take up or Occupancy Indicators

Take up indicators show the level of use of a service, (eg numbers of people registered for an evening class) or the extent to which a service is used compared to its maximum occupancy level (eg number of hostel beds available in a month compared to numbers actually resident in a month).

## 3. Impact or Result Indicators

Result indicators aim to show the effect of the service, by collecting data on what difference or benefit occurred from using the service. For example, within three months of attending a return to work course, 40% of the students went into some kind of employment.

## 4. User reactions

User reactions record the degree of satisfaction that users have as a result of using a service, for example an analysis of complaints received could be one possible indicator.

There are two important considerations in developing indicators: the ability to collect the information, and the type of system that will be used to collect it.

There are a number of different ways of collecting performance measurement information. This is an example for a centre providing counselling support to families.

Box 3.2

## Ways of collecting performance management information

**Information that is relatively easy to collect**

Take up indicators
*numbers attending each session*

Client reactions
(immediately after using service)
*post- interview satisfaction questionnaire*

**Closed statistical method** —— **Open methods**

Comparative analysis
*comparing the effectiveness of similar centres*

*comparing other courses of action open to the families*

Longer- term client feedback
*asking ex-clients about the benefit they gained from using the centre*

**information that is difficult to collect**

In the example, the counselling centre's **take up indicators** were fairly easy to collect as the staff kept a simple daily log which could easily be collated into a monthly statistical report.

It is often very hard to develop **comparative analysis** as no two providers of the same service are ever identical. Either complex negotiations would be needed to ensure that the comparison was fair and fully takes into account local circumstances, or the comparison would have to be based on information and data chosen in an arbitrary manner. To enable data to be analysed, it is likely that the information would have to be collected in a statistical format.

The **client reaction** analysis involved asking clients to fill in a short questionnaire which asked a mixture of "open" questions (such as "what do you like/dislike about the centre") and "closed" questions (such as "would you recommend this centre to anyone with a similar problem: yes/no"). As such this is a relatively easy thing to do. However, given that the questionnaire asks for comments and opinions, analysis was time consuming.

The centre's **longer term client feedback** involved contacting clients three months after their case "ended" and asking them to complete a form saying what they thought of the service offered and how they might have directly or indirectly benefited from it. This information was harder to collect (since there is always likely to be a low response to postal questionnaires), and analysis had to be of an open and discursive nature .

One interesting issue was that the views that clients had about the service changed throughout their involvement in the centre. Many were unsure of what to expect when they first were referred to the centre. In the early stages of counselling it was not unusual for clients to feel resistant to some of the processes involved. It was often not until the later stages that clients fully understood the processes used by the centre. This would need to be taken into account in any attempt to find out users views.

# Agreeing performance measures

The process of negotiating and agreeing performance measurement is often rushed. There are numerous examples of local authority officers working under pressure to bring in a performance measurement system to a tight timetable and not having the time available to think through what information is needed or useful. Many voluntary sector managers also have experience of committing their agency to performance indicators which they hope that they can meet as part of a making a "good impression" in a funding application.

# Designing performance measures

The box below suggests a model for designing and using useful performance measures and gives an example of how it works:

Box 3.3

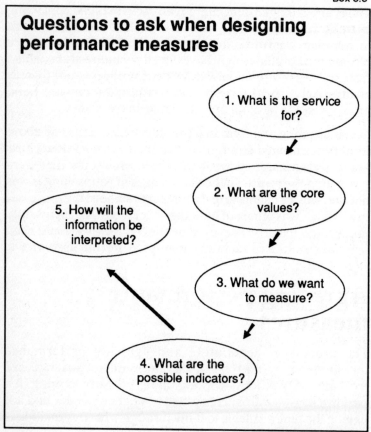

## Questions to ask when designing performance measures

1. What is the service for?

2. What are the core values?

3. What do we want to measure?

4. What are the possible indicators?

5. How will the information be interpreted?

## Stage 1:
# What is the service for?

This stage involves identifying what the purpose of the service is. What needs does it intend to meet? Why was it set up?

All performance measures should be firmly based on the long term aims and specific objectives of the organisation. In agreeing performance indicators with funders it is important to reach a shared understanding of the organisation's purpose and values.

## Stage 2:
# What are the core values?

Values are the key principles and ways of working that are central to an organisation's existence. Possible values might include, working with low income members of the community or equal opportunities in service delivery or a commitment to client rights. It therefore makes sense that whatever measures are used reflect the organisation's core values.

It is important that performance indicators measure the things that an organisation regards as important and are distinctive about its style and method of working. It could be argued that how an organisation works with its clients is as important as how many clients it works with. Core values should then be reflected in any monitoring and review process.

## Stage 3:
# What do we want to measure?

From clarifying what the service is intended to do and identifying the core values that should guide how it operates the organisation should be in a position to work out what aspects of it should be measured.

At this stage, the expectations of funding bodies will need to be considered. Hopefully funding bodies will share the points that emerge from stages 1 and 2. However it is possible that they will only want indicators which give basic information about minimum levels of performance (eg numbers of people using the service). Negotiators will have to decide whether to include alongside these "bottom line" indicators, ones which also describe the performance of the organisation in meeting its long term aims and working in a way which enhances its values.

## Stage 4:
# What are the possible indicators?

After listing what it is to be measured, the next stage is to decide upon the most appropriate and cost efficient method of collecting the required information, data and views.

The extra cost and time likely to be spent on collecting and compiling the information needs to be calculated. Is this a reasonable use of limited resources?

## Stage 5:
# How will the information be interpreted?

It is really very easy to interpret a simple piece of information in many different ways. The case study on page 25 illustrates this point. Discussion should focus on what interpretation could be made on information and data collected under each indicator.

# Interpreting the information

It may be that a funding body has a view on what minimum standard each indicator should have. A disability group was asked to compile statistics on how many people used its resource centre every day. The group was surprised to hear informally that the monitoring officer (who had little real knowledge of the group or its clients) regarded twenty users per day as being acceptable and that any fall below twenty was regarded as "poor performance". At no stage had this been discussed openly.

Box 3.4

# Case study: a question of interpretation

Two information offices provide a similar service and with the same levels of staffing. A performance measurement system was developed using two indicators

• How many people used the centre in a month.

• The average length of each interview.

The figures reveal that Centre A had 75 clients calling in for initial interviews and that the average interview lasted 10 minutes while staff at Centre B saw 38 clients and the average interview lasted 30 minutes.

The following very different interpretations could be placed on this information.

*"Centre A is obviously busier as it sees more people."*

*"Centre A is better than Centre B as it can deal with more people in an efficient (i.e. quick) way."*

*"Centre B is probably dis-organised as it takes on average 20 minutes longer to provide the same information as centre A."*

*"Centre B gives callers more time. People probably get a much more personalised and responsive service than at centre A."*

*"I suspect that many of Centre A's callers are repeat visits i.e. the same people coming back again. If more time was spent with them initially, as probably happens at Centre B, it would be more efficient in the longer term."*

*"On average Centre A staff conducted 12.5 hours of initial interviews. Centre B staff conducted 19 hours of interviews. That means that Centre B staff work harder and are busier."*

It is advisable to check with the officers who might be interpreting collected information if they have any formal or informal yardstick of what is poor, acceptable or good performance.

Most performance review systems do not have an explicit statement of what kind of interpretation will be placed on the collected information. It may be appropriate to agree to a regular review meeting to look at trends and patterns that emerge from indicators, discuss possible interpretations and identify future action.

The case study in box 3.4 shows just how easy it is to draw from a relatively simple piece of information very different and, in fact, contradictory conclusions. The collection of average times tell little, if anything about the quality of the interview and the long term effectiveness of it.

In looking at any set of information we usually interpret it based upon sets of assumptions and personal beliefs about what we think is the right way to do something.

Clearly it is important to clarify how managers, funders and staff will interpret whatever information a performance indicator produces. What assumptions will they be making in "judging" the information?

Box 3.5

---

# A checklist for performance indicators

Are the performance indicators:

- ❏ Related to a specific function or activity
- ❏ Capable of control or being improved
- ❏ Measurable
- ❏ Related to the values and objectives of the project
- ❏ Agreed in advance

Is the information:

- ❏ Easy to collect
- ❏ Easy to understand
- ❏ Linked into the planning
- ❏ Giving a clear and total picture
- ❏ Cost effective to collect

---

# Choosing the right indicators

The following points should be considered in drawing up a range of performance indicators:

## Are they related to a specific function or activity?

It makes sense that indicators directly relate to the way in which the organisation is structured. Indicators should not cut across staff teams or budget heads. They should relate as much as is possible to the way in which the organisation organises its services and activities. It should be clear which part of the organisation or which individual is responsible for managing the activity that the performance indicator reports on.

A community health project with seven staff could choose to design groups of indicators either around its three main programmes;

- Education resource centre.
- HIV campaign.
- Drugs work.

Or for the three "teams" its staff work in:

- Admin and information team
- Outreach team.
- Promotions team

It would have to decide which structure would give it, and probably its funders, the most useful information.

## Are they capable of control or of being improved?

There is no point in being measured against something which the organisation is not actually responsible for or is not capable of improving or managing better.

A voluntary group working with young homeless people is not responsible for the numbers of homeless young people in its town (in fact their work might well establish that there are more young homeless people than previously estimated). Using the numbers of young people homeless in a town as an indicator of performance (as opposed to an indicator of need) is pointless and unfair.

Changes in the social security system might mean that a welfare rights worker has less opportunity to win a direct increase in a person's benefit, however hard she works. So using "successful outcomes" (i.e. winning a case) as an indicator might well provide interesting information, but, not necessarily on the performance of a welfare rights service.

It is useful to ask "can we actually improve in any way the performance that is being monitored or is it entirely dependant on external circumstances beyond our influence?".

## Are they measurable?

Performance review can only focus on things that are measurable in either quantity or quality terms. Are there aspects of the service which are important, but, are particularly difficult to measure? Or where the costs or time involved in collecting data would be too much?

Could the process of collecting information be objected to or cause suspicion amongst clients or users?

## Are they related to values and objectives?

Do the performance indicators actually measure what the organisation (and hopefully its funders) regards as important about what it does and how it does it?

If the organisation has any forward plan with specific objectives do the performance indicators record progress and developments in meeting the plan?

## Are they agreed in advance?

Performance measures should not be imposed retrospectively It is unfair for a funding body to ask for performance measurement information at the end of a funding agreement unless it has been requested at the start. Agreeing indicators in advance allows the organisation to implement systems to collect information and by monitoring performance throughout the period be able to intervene to improve performance.

## Are they easy to collect?

There is much more likelihood of a performance measurement system being effective and accurate if the recording system is easy to use. Wherever possible any recording system should be integrated into current procedures such as booking systems, casework record systems or diaries rather than staff having to fill in separate monitoring systems.

## Are they easy to understand?

The information collected together should be in an easy to read and simple format. There is a tendency from some funding bodies, to restrict information to a few core statistics to make analysis and compilation easy.

Any statistical information should be collected in such a way whereby, if it is necessary, it can be accompanied by some commentary which describes any significant factors (eg. . . . "February figures are lower than usual because the building was closed for re-decoration work for three days"). This might make the process of compiling the information more difficult to structure, but should prevent ill informed judgements being made.

## Are they linked into planning?

There should be a link between collecting information about performance and making decisions about an organisation's short and long term future. Trends and data gleaned from the performance measurement system should be used to inform decisions about budgets and future plans (for example if a group is unable to meet its performance standard that the office is always open from 10. 00 to 16. 00 it might need to consider how it organises staff cover).

## Do they give an even and total picture?

Some parts of an organisation are easier to measure than other parts. There is a danger of only focusing on the tangible (... how many people and at what cost?) aspects of the organisation and ignoring things that are intangible (often intangible things are about the way an organisation works, eg does it consult its clients, does it give choices) or might seem to be incidental. The range of indicators agreed should reflect the full scope, depth and purpose of the organisation.

## Are they cost effective?

How much will it cost to record and collect the information? How much staff time will it take up? Is the value that will hopefully be gained from collecting information about performance worth the cost and time involved in collecting it?

# Examples of performance indicators

*Indicator*                *Description and comments*

$$\frac{\text{Cost of service}}{\text{Number of times used}}$$

UNIT COST          **Description:** The overall cost of an activity is divided by the number of times it is used in a fixed time. So, for example, it might cost £32,000 per quarter to run a home visiting service. If during this period the agency carries out 960 home visits, the unit cost (the average cost of a visit) is £33.

**Comments:** Unit costs are popular with managers and accountants in the public sector, particularly the Health Service. They are of value in controlling costs and seeing trends, but they say little, if anything, about the quality and effectiveness of a service.

| Indicator | Description and comments |
|-----------|--------------------------|

Total admin and central costs
_____
Cost of activities and projects

**COST OF OVERHEADS AGAINST THE OUTPUTS**

**Description:** This indicator sets the cost of an organisation's administration and management functions against the cost of each service. An agency might be able to show that 26% of its income goes on administration and central resources (eg the building).

**Comments:**This indicator leaves itself open to "creative accounting"... deciding what to apportion as a central cost is an important decision in itself.

**COMPARISON INDICATOR**

**Description:** The relevant costs and performance of one organisation is compared to another similar organisation. For example, a housing association might compare its average rent levels against those in neighbouring associations. Sometimes it can be used to create a "league table" of the performance of similar organisations.

**Comments:**Comparison indicators have been popular with the government as part of creating a "market" where people can choose between services. There is often a major difficulty in making a fair comparison. Organisations invariably organise themselves differently, local needs and local costs are inclined to vary considerably.

31

| Indicator | Description and comments |
|---|---|

Optimum Use
—————————
Actual Use

**OCCUPANCY RATE**

**Description:** An occupancy indicator compares the optimum possible use within a period against the actual use. So for example a training centre might be available for use for 40 sessions in a month, if it is only used for 35 sessions the occupancy rate is 87.5%.

**Comments:** There can be some difficulties in establishing what is the optimum figure. If an occupancy rate indicator is used then the person compiling it must be able to add comments explaining patterns of use.

**TAKE UP RATE**

**Description:** The number of people using a service. This type of indicator is to record the numbers of clients or users taking part in a specific activity. It is used frequently in areas such as training (numbers of people attending a course) or in advice work (numbers of enquires per month).

**Comments:** There is some obvious value in measuring the extent to which a service is used. However, this indicator says little about the quality or the users perception of the service. There is a tendency to ask further questions about the profile of users (eg. ethnic origin, age, geographic area etc) this can be very useful, but, can sometimes be regarded as intrusive or unnecessarily bureaucratic by users.

| Indicator | Description and comments |
|---|---|

**PERFORMANCE AGAINST AN AGREED STANDARD**

**Description:** An organisation commits itself to operating a service to an advertised standard (eg. all enquires will be acknowledged in three working days or that the office will always be staffed from 09.30 to 17.00 every day). It then monitors to ensure that the standard is kept to.

**Comments:** This indicator can only really be used for the tangible aspects of an organisation's work (waiting times, response times, range of services etc). The information should be presented in such a way that staff are able to add comments to explain why standards are not met.

**PERFORMANCE AGAINST AN AGREED PLAN**

**Description:** An organisation, team or individual draws up a plan setting out how they intend to use their time, what objectives they will have and what kind of outputs they hope to produce. At the end of the period achievements are measured against the plan.

**Comments:** This kind of indicator often has some managerial benefit by helping teams and individuals to clarify short and long term objectives. There is a danger of a plan becoming inflexible (particularly in work such as community development, which, because of its participatory and responsive nature is often difficult to plan precisely). One possible solution is only to plan say 70% of time and thus allow some flexible time which can be recorded separately. It is important that staff are allowed to design systems for planning that accurately reflect their work.

| Type of indicator | Description and comments |
|---|---|
| | **Description:** The immediate reaction of users and clients through the collection of reactions, opinions and complaints during and after a users involvement with a service. |
| USER FEEDBACK | **Comments:** User feedback can provide some very useful information. Often people are reluctant to comment openly on services that they use or depend on. Thought needs to be given to the most effective ways of gathering this information. The views of non users or people who were users, but, drifted away, could also be gathered to provide comparative information. |
| A COMMUNI-CATIONS AUDIT | **Description:** An audit of the organisations users or potential users to find out what they know about the organisation and its services. It might also be valuable to ask other agencies that the organisation works with to describe what they see as the organisations role and services. |
| | **Comments:** Useful way of finding out what people think what the organisation is for and checking that the organisation's public relations and communications is working. |

| *Indicator* | *Description and comments* |
| --- | --- |
| **MONITORING VISITS** | **Description:** Visits formal or informal, planned or spontaneous by funding officers to the agency to see it in operation and monitor performance. |
| | **Comments:** Often a very subjective process. Unless visits have a structure and clear purpose they can, at best give a vague impression of how it works on the day of the visit and at worst can interrupt the work of staff. This kind of visit has now been elevated into a management theory. . . . MBWA. . . management by wandering around. |
| **CASE REVIEWS AND AUDITS** | **Description:** A detailed analysis of a number of cases to ensure that the case has been managed in accordance with agreed standards and practice. |
| | **Comments:** There is a potential danger of breaching guarantees of confidentiality. There may be ways of involving the client in evaluating their reactions and experience. |
| **FOLLOW UP REVIEWS** | **Description:** A random sample of users are contacted after they have used the service and asked to comment on what they gained by using the service and their opinion of the way that the service is organised |
| | **Comments:** Often provide very useful information. An attempt to measure "outcomes" as well as outputs. Can be time consuming or difficult to organise. |

| Indicator | Description and comments |
|---|---|

**NEGATIVE INDICATOR**

**Description:** The recording of incidents when performance falls below a particular standard or target. For example, a housing association has a policy of being able to re-let a property from when it becomes vacant in x days. Every time it is unable to do this (i.e. it takes longer than x days) would be recorded by the negative indicator.

**Comments:** Negative indicators can be difficult to monitor and collect as a degree of trust is necessary. Negative indicators can be useful as an "alarm bell system" to point out where managers need to intervene or where extra resources might be needed.

**MATCHING PRE-EXPECTATION WITH POST-EXPERIENCE**

**Description:** Users of a service are surveyed to find out what they want or expect from a service before they use it. They are then surveyed after using it and their experience is analysed against their expectations. For example, before joining a training programme participants are surveyed to establish their needs and expectations; three months later they are then asked to evaluate the course.

**Comments:** Can be a complex form of measurement as it relies on descriptive comments which can make analysis difficult. It needs to be recognised that it is acceptable for participants original expectations not to have been met, but they may have still gained something useful and positive.

| Indicator | Description and comments |
|---|---|

**COMPLAINTS ANALYSIS**

**Description:** An analysis of complaints recorded during a specific period. The analysis should be in such a form that trends and particular problems can be easily identified.

**Comments:** A useful method. It can be argued that the fact that users are taking the trouble to make a complaint is actually a positive indicator that they have some confidence that the service is capable of managing itself better and is capable of offering redress.

**RESPONSE / TURNAROUND TIME**

**Description:** The time it takes to respond to something is measured and analysed. For example, the average time to process a grant application could be measured every month and compared against previous months.

**Comments:** Response time indicators need to be used alongside other indicators that look at quality issues. On occasions when response/turnaround indicators have been used in isolation there has often been an increase in errors as staff take "shortcuts" in order to respond quickly.

Box 3.5

# Performance indicators – some "good" examples

Numerous performance indicators have been thrown together in a hurry, that only count the things that are easy to count and ignore the things that are important. The indicators listed below are possible "positive" ones which could meet an organisation's specific values and objectives:

## 1. Staff Training and Development

A simple indicator showing the average number of training days attend. A second indicator could record the total amount spent on staff development as a percentage of the total salary budget.

These indicators could be used as a measure of good management practice and also of a commitment to maintain high professional standards

## 2. Consultation with users

An indicator that records total number of staff hours or days spent on consulting with users, non users and past users on the quality of services and in the planning of future services.

## 3. Independent "audit" of cases

A review of randomly selected closed cases by an outside expert to evaluate the accuracy of casework and to discuss with the caseworker and also the client the effectiveness of the approach taken.

## 4. An indicator of "unmet" need

Compiling a list of occasions when an agency has had to turn people away, either because the service has reached a capacity level or because the needs expressed could not be met by the agency's current services.

## 5. An action report on specific measures taken to improve services in line with agreed policies.

For example:

*Policy Objective:* To improve access for people with disabilities.

*Action taken:* During this quarter we have:

• Met with the councils disability adviser to review access.

• Established the cost of an appropriate wheelchair lift.

Box 3.5 continued

• Met with local disabled groups to discuss access needs.

*Policy Objective:* To work in a way that reflects good environmental practice

*Action taken:*

• Reviewed all purchasing policies.

• Arranged for a heating audit to be carried out.

## 6. Innovative or developmental projects

An agency that is committed to finding new solutions to problems could record, as an indicator, what new projects or activities it is involved in as a measure of its innovative work and developmental role.

Box 3.6

# Performance indicators: dials or tin openers?

Neil Carter, writing in Policy and Politics in 1989 comments on a trend in central government to look for precise measures of performance when there are very few available. "It is helpful to think of performance indicators as being used either as dials or as tin openers. Implicit in the use of performance indicators as dials is the assumption that standards of performance are unambiguous, implicit in the use of performance indicators as tin openers is the assumption that performance is a contestable notion."

Thinking of indicators as dials assumes that the information is always clear and correct (like the speed of a car shown on the speedometer). However, there are few things that can always be measured with such accuracy. Thinking of performance indicators as tin openers recognises that most performance measurement systems of any value, raise more questions than provide precise answers.

# Summary

1. How will you be able to limit the number of possible indicators that you could develop and concentrate on a limited number of indicators that provide valuable information?

2. Do the measures that you intend to use really give an even picture of your work? Do they report on the things that you (and hopefully, your funder) regard as important?

3. What interpretation is being placed on the information gathered by the indicators?

4. Do the indicators measure the quality aspects of what you do as well as the quantity element?

# Hill Street Community Centre
## >> the continuing story

The community centre received most of its income from the local authority in the form of an annual grant. In November every year, Hilary had to fill in a form saying how much they needed and what they were going to use it for. It was not a particularly difficult task.

This year things were different. The newly appointed Director of Community Services had recommended to the council that it should adopt a system of performance measures for all voluntary organisations and in the long term, move towards a contractual relationship with voluntary groups.

A new form was circulated to all voluntary groups. It asked for "specific performance indicators" for all areas receiving funding. Hilary took the new form home and spent a weekend guessing at what kind of information the council wanted. For example, for the centre's two minibuses, Hilary noted down a range of things that could be counted – number of passengers number of trips, number of days out of action, types of groups booking the minibus.

On Monday, Hilary telephoned the officer in the grants unit (now called "The external services development unit") who normally liaised with the centre. Hilary explained that the centre had been able to list 52 separate indicators for its work. Was this enough? How was Hilary going to get it all on the application form?

The officer reluctantly explained that he had not a clue what kind of indicators were needed or what was to be done with the information collected by them. All he knew was that neither he nor councillors had discovered any extra time to look at them. He suggested that Hilary sent "in something short that looks right".

For her minibuses, Hilary decided to record the total mileage (which she had from the service books), and, as an afterthought, tried working out the average cost per journey.

Hilary decided not to ask if the external services development unit was using performance indicators to measure the effectiveness of its own work.

# Chapter 4
# VALUE FOR MONEY

A Chartered Institute of Public Finance and Accountancy Publication (CIPFA) on Value For Money sums up the confusion and misuse of the term "value for money".

"Few slogans can have been so widely adopted and yet be so misunderstood as 'value for money'. It has been variously used as a political rallying call; as a euphemism for expenditure reductions; and to imply quality and cheapness in goods as diverse as motor cars and washing up liquids. It was coined from within the public sector finance discipline to give expression to a prime economic goal of most public service organisations." (Reprinted with the permission of the Chartered Institute of Public Finance and Accountancy)

A commonly accepted definition of Value for Money is based around

## The three E's

- Economy
- Efficiency
- Effectiveness

The three E's are usually defined as follows:

# 1. Economy

Economy is the actual cost of the activity.

What is the cost of the service taking into account the various inputs (money, equipment, time etc)?.

Could the same quality of service be provided in a more economic (or cheaper) way?

Is their proper control of resources?

Is good management, housekeeping and thrift practised?

# 2. Efficiency

Efficiency is the relationship between the costs involved in providing a service (i.e. the inputs) and what the service produces (i.e. the outputs).

If it was organised and managed better could the same output be produced with less input, or could more outputs be produced with the same input?

Is the maximum output being achieved from the input?

Are the direct and indirect costs to the public reasonable compared to other providers?

# 3. Effectiveness

Effectiveness is an attempt to measure the benefit or longer term value of a service or activity.

Did it actually do what it said it would?

What is the longer term benefit?

Are there any "side effects" or wider implications?

Does the service meet its stated objectives?

# Points about value for money

## Does it reflect social priorities?

There has been discussion within the voluntary sector about the ability of the value for money concept to take into account social commitments such as "to work with the groups that are socially or economically disadvantaged" or to "target groups who usually find services less accessible".

For example, a home-care agency which makes some charge for its services could, by directing its services at people with more disposable income, "score" better under a Value For Money audit as extra income could subsidise the service and so reduce its cost to the funder.

Often, some groups in a society are harder to work with than others. It may well be cheaper to run a minibus service in a city area than in a rural area with a scattered population. Some clients might be "cheaper" (i.e. less demanding or less intensive) to work with than others.

Does value for money take into account a commitment to equal provision and social equity.

## Is it all about the "money" and not the "value"?

Money is tangible and can easily be identified and recorded. The value of a service is often not immediately obvious and can be hard to accurately identify. Commentators on Value for Money such as the National Consumers Council have observed that value for money studies have "degenerated. . . . attention is generally paid only to economy and efficiency". The quality of the value of the service is ignored.

## Does economy mean "doing things on the cheap"?

It is easy to focus on finding ways of making short term cuts which simply create long term problems. Value for money should be about providing a service in such a way that makes short and long term economic sense.

It could be argued that many voluntary groups have either consistently under-estimated the costs of their activities or because of lack of funds failed to properly invest and have ran services at very low cost. Box 4.3 on page 49 gives some examples of this.

## Is it about increasing output rather than achieving quality?

Value for money uses a "production" model of inputs, outputs and outcomes. How appropriate is this? Is its aim to increase the volume of the service at the possible expense of the quality?

## How does it relate to innovative projects?

A traditional strength of the voluntary sector is its ability and willingness to experiment and try new ways of doing things. This invariably involves an element of risk that a project might not deliver what was originally hoped for.

Innovation is increasingly recognised as important, but a narrow value for money study would not be impressed by an innovative project that, despite hard work, did not pay off in outputs.

## What is the link between efficiency and effectiveness?

Management writers such as Peter Drucker, have stressed that unless an organisation thinks strategically about its purpose it can very easily do entirely the wrong thing in a very efficient manner.

Just because a service is run in an efficient way it does not mean it is effective in delivering the "right services to the right people".

Box 4.2

# Example of a value for money study

This example shows how the terms "economy" "efficiency" and "effectiveness" might be used in measuring a local voluntary organisation. The Carebreak agency provides a support service for people caring for elderly relatives at home. It has a main office and a sub office in the northern part of town. It employs three staff, assisted by a team of regular volunteers. It provides the following services:

• A respite service to give carers an occasional break.

• Practical support and advice eg. help with shopping, advice on benefits etc.

• Social and informal support networks.

A value for money study of Carebreak takes the following approach:

## 1. ECONOMY

Can the service be run in a way that provides the same level and quality of service, but at less cost, by another agency?

Are the costs involved in funding this agency similar to those involved in funding other services which can be identified as being a reasonable comparison?

Do rents and wage levels seem reasonable when compared against local market trends and the "local rate for the job"?

Does the organisation have a sensible purchasing policy for the various supplies it needs? Would it be better to purchase outright, rent or lease the office equipment and the mini bus?

Are there adequate systems of financial control to properly control spending and ensure that money is used properly?

## 2. EFFICIENCY

Is there any way of improving the organisation of the service so as to take on more clients and provide the same quality of service without directly increasing costs?

How does having a separate sub office affect the output? Could more services be delivered if the staff all worked from one office?

Is the way in which the service is organised such that the best possible use is made of all resources?

Box 4.2 continued

**3. EFFECTIVENESS**

Has the service done what it said it would do?

- What benefit has been gained as a result of the service?
- Has it provided a service of a consistent "quality"?
- What are the long term effects of the service?

Does the recorded level of mistakes, errors and complaints indicate that the service is failing to meet its objectives?

What is the user profile of the service? Is it directing its services to the people who need it most? How does it decide who to work with?

**What outcomes is the service achieving?**

One further approach for an organisation like Carebreak to take would be to compare the cost of providing its service to the likely costs involved if the service was not available. It could be argued that if Carebreak was not available, it is likely that some of the carers would not be able to carry on and that the person being cared for at home would probably have to go into residential care and probably cost public funds considerably more.

# What is the link between short term and long term?

Economy and efficiency can usually be measured in the short term (eg within a financial year). The effectiveness of a service, particularly ones involved in providing some element of social care or community development might not become apparent for a number of years. Preventative work often has a considerable initial cost, but it can only be valued if the long term cost of not doing it is estimated.

# Effectiveness is often hard to measure

The effectiveness of a service might be valued differently by the funder and the user. Effectiveness is often a matter of "perception" rather than objective measurement.

A further complication is that there is not always a direct line between outputs and outcomes. An organisation might produce "high quality" services which are used in an entirely different way by a local community. They place a value on that service, but it is different from the one originally intended.

## The link between effectiveness and cost

If a service is effective (i.e. it is of a consistent quality that meets people's needs) then it can be assumed that it will possibly attract new users or that existing users will keep using it and that their expectations of it will rise. Being effective can mean that a service is used more and therefore costs (either on a unit or an overall basis) are likely to rise and thus the "economic" element will change.

If a community centre is well managed and is responding to local needs in a popular and effective way its resources will come under greater strain. At the very least, it will need more cleaning, maintaining, administration and management. Its equipment will be used more often and will probably need servicing and repairing more often than a quieter centre.

Is the way in which value for money is used sophisticated enough to recognise this link?

# Making comparisons

Value for money is only of any consequence if it can be used to make comparisons between organisations or services. Without something to compare the results of a value for money study against, it is of little practical use.

In the public sector the Chartered Institute of Public Finance and Accountancy (CIPFA) and the Audit Commission have both tried to group similar local authorities together in "clusters" so that comparisons can be made. This is a difficult and sometimes controversial exercise. No two service providers are ever identical either in terms of their internal organisation and objectives or in the external environment in which they operate. History, user profiles, local socio-economic factors are all variables which make finding a relatively exact comparison difficult.

Box 4.3

# Voluntary organisations and uneconomic practices

It is possible to use value for money as a positive negotiating argument by suggesting that some activities are run in an "uneconomic" way because they have been underfunded.

The policy of doing things "on the cheap" does not make sense from a value for money point of view.

The following are some examples of "uneconomic" practices:

● By paying lower wages than similar employers the organisation either fails to recruit good staff or recruits good staff who leave quickly, as they can get better salaries elsewhere. A high turnover of staff – caused by poor salary levels – may well increase costs when recruitment costs and allowing time for new staff to learn their new roles are taken into account.

● An organisation may fail to "invest in the infrastructure". It does not make for good value for money if staff are regularly prevented from doing their proper job because they have to spend too much time on basic administrative tasks. Not allowing for proper administrative support or using labour saving technology works against effective management.

● If an organisation is unable to fund staff training and development, the quality and efficiency of the service could suffer, staff could become demoralised and their performance less effective as their skills become out of date.

Value for money is not about doing something for the cheapest short term cost. Indeed, it could be argued that a value for money approach for some organisations might actually require an initial investment of more money to allow effective and efficient practices to be implemented.

The types of comparisons that can be made include:

● Is the service provided on a cheaper basis elsewhere?

● Are more services delivered this year compared to last year?

● Do similar organisations manage to provide the same services at less cost?

Is there a measurable longer term difference to clients or districts that have had the benefit of this service compared to similar clients or districts that have not? If so, is the difference of such a value that it was worth the original cost?

Could the same value be achieved by providing a different (and possibly cheaper) service?

Is this the most cost effective way of providing a service? If it were provided in a different way (eg through contracting it out or doing it "in house") would it provide better value for money?

## Summary

1. Is Value for Money as a concept broad enough to include all of the aspects of your services and activities?

2. Whose criteria is being used to assess "value"?

3. If your performance is being compared to another organisation, how reasonable a comparison is it?

# Hill Street Community Centre
## >> *the continuing story*

The council's financial crisis was now an annual event rather like Christmas. Rumours of budget cuts would spread and spending would be frozen. However this year it seemed much more serious. The council's treasurer explained that his repertoire of creative accounting tricks was now exhausted.

Council committees set about drawing up action plans to identify savings. The Community Recreation Committee decided to ask its officers to carry out an "efficiency review of voluntary groups that it funds to ensure that they provide value for money".

Two council officers arrived at Hill Street Community Centre to review its operation as part of the review. They spent a day asking about purchasing arrangements, occupancy levels, financial control systems, income generation and the potential for more work with other agencies on the same estate.

The officers were reasonable people. Their questions ranged from simple administrative ones about how the centre managed the few resources it had to very searching ones about why did the centre choose to run a particular service in a particular way. Hilary, the centre's co-ordinator, began to suspect that they did not exactly know what they were looking to find.

Before the officers left to write up their report, one of them admitted that carrying out a review of a community centre was very different from previous projects they had been involved with. It was relatively easy to do a value for money audit of say, the council's vehicle repair depot – it was easy to make direct comparisons, the purpose of the depot was easy to define and therefore measuring its performance was straightforward. The community centre activities were not organised in a neat and tidy way, the long term value of its activities were often hard to accurately record and it was very difficult to identify any other centre that did the same things to make a fair comparison with.

The whole process set Hilary thinking . . What is the centre supposed to be doing? How can the centre evaluate its work? How can it identify what value it adds to the local estate and who should determine the criteria by which its work should be judged?

# Chapter 5

# A QUESTION OF QUALITY

"Quality" is now a firmly established concept in the management process of health and social care agencies. Social service departments and Health Authorities have appointed Quality Assurance managers. Quality has been adopted as a central objective in central and local government policy. The creation of local authority inspection units with the brief of ensuring quality of service is an important development. Many statutory and voluntary organisations have embarked on a process of developing quality assurance systems and have experimented with different systems and techniques.

This chapter explains what is meant by quality, looks at its background and the main concepts that underpin it and outlines a possible approach to developing a quality model.

The main concepts behind "quality management" have their roots in manufacturing industry's rapid development (particularly in Japan and in the United States) of new technological and manufacturing processes. To identify the "quality elements" in areas such as social care or community development requires considerable effort and careful thought, although advocates of a quality approach would argue that it has substantial benefit.

Box5.1

# A guide to quality speak

## Total Quality Management

Total Quality Management or TQM is a management process that focuses on identifying how all aspects of a process (suppliers, managers, front line staff and support staff) directly contribute to the quality of a product or service. It stresses the importance of team work, systems, communication and continual improvement to ensure that quality standards are always met.

## Quality Assurance

A term increasingly used in the field of social and health care. Essentially it involves designing and planning services in a way that guarantees that the service will always meet the agreed standard. Systems and indicators need to be developed to ensure that the service consistently operates to its agreed standards. Quality Assurance should be a "pro-active" management process.

## Quality Control

A process directed at inspecting a process after it has been completed and checking that it is acceptable. It is more of a "re-active" or "firefighting" process than quality assurance.

## The Cost of Quality

The direct and indirect cost of making mistakes and having to correct work later.

## BS5750, EN 29000 and IS9000

Externally accredited certifications showing that an organisation has in place systems and processes to measure and ensure a quality product or service. BS5750 is the UK standard, EN 29000 the European one and IS9000 the international one. All follow the same pattern and format.

Box 5.1 continued

## Statistical Process Control

A preventative method to ensure that at each step of a process staff check their own work against agreed standards to ensure that it conforms to standard. Statistical Process Control should give staff the "feedback" on what is happening so that they can take action if things start to fall below standard.

## Quality Circles

A management and communication strategy, originally developed in Japanese industry, whereby, groups of workers meet on a regular basis to identify ways in which services can be improved.

Defining the term "quality" is the starting point. Often it is assumed that quality means "excellence" – providing the "best" possible or most expensive service or product. Sometimes discussions about quality simply see it as being an "end of the line" inspection or quality control function. Writers and experts on quality would disagree and define quality in terms such as:

● A systematic approach to ensure that the product or service consistently does what it is supposed to do.

● A service being "fit for its purpose or use".

● Effectively responding to and meeting a users needs.

The following processes need to be undertaken to develop a quality assurance system:

● Consultation and research with the "end user" (client, customer etc. . . . ) to find out what they regard as the important quality elements of the service. It may be useful to talk to "non users" to find out if there are any blocks or barriers that discourage or prevent them from using a service.

● With this information and with input from the staff who carry out the service a number of measurable "quality standards" should be developed setting out in clear terms how the service should operate.

- The current service (both what it does and how it does it) should be evaluated to see how it measures up against the quality standards. Strategies to bring the service up to standards should be agreed, costed and planned.

- A detailed analysis of all of the elements involved in providing a service to ensure that everything is organised in an effective and efficient way will need to be undertaken. This usually involves tracing all the different activities in providing a service, ensuring that they understand the needs of the user and that they fit together in a logical way. This process of improving the relationships within an organisation and creating better teamwork is called building a "service chain".

- The organisation will need to invest in staff training, job reviews, and the development of systems and procedures to ensure that the standards are capable of being monitored and consistently met.

## After the quality assurance system is launched

Once a quality assurance system has been launched, managers need to focus on four issues:

- Providing continual support, training and assistance to staff to enable them to provide a quality service.

- Monitoring the service to ensure that it is meeting its standards and intervening to resolve any problems or take preventative action.

- Consulting with users to check that their expectations are being met and identify new trends or needs that may lead to the revision of standards.

- Identifying ways of improving the service and possibly raising the standards. Users expectations are inclined to rise as the quality of a service goes up.

Box 5.2

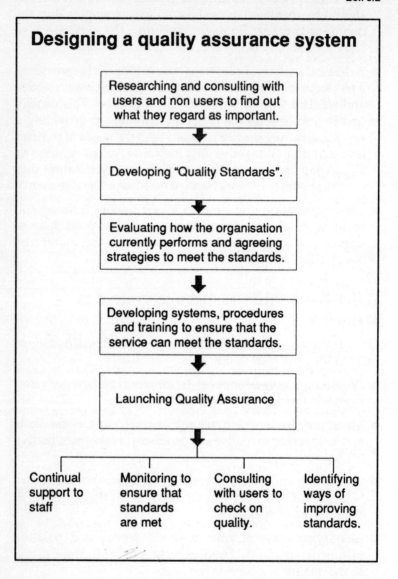

**Designing a quality assurance system**

Researching and consulting with users and non users to find out what they regard as important.

Developing "Quality Standards".

Evaluating how the organisation currently performs and agreeing strategies to meet the standards.

Developing systems, procedures and training to ensure that the service can meet the standards.

Launching Quality Assurance

| Continual support to staff | Monitoring to ensure that standards are met | Consulting with users to check on quality. | Identifying ways of improving standards. |

# The implications of introducing a quality assurance system

Developing a quality assurance system demands considerable time and effort from all parts of an organisation. It can have a number of useful benefits.

- It focuses on the needs, aspirations and experiences of the service user. It should provide a better service and enable the users to articulate their needs more effectively.

- It can cut costs by eliminating unnecessary functions and bureaucratic processes. The emphasis is on finding out why things go wrong and developing systems and processes that "get things right first time". The cost of errors is rarely counted. A considerable amount of most managers time is spent reacting to things that repeatedly go wrong. Quality Assurance is about managing in a pro-active way.

- Having quality assurance systems in place (and possibly having them approved through an accreditation process such as BS5750) can improve the standing and credibility of the organisation in the eyes of other institutions that it is negotiating agreements or contracts with.

To develop a quality assurance system an organisation needs to focus on two fundamental questions:

- How do we find out about the needs, aspirations and expectations of the people who use our services?

- Do we really know who our users are? How do we describe the relationship? Are they clients, customers, users, consumers, members, or partners? What status and rights do they have?

In analysing the service and trying to define service standards the following issues are often raised.

- Staff doing the identical job may perform it in very different ways, with a different style and a different level of competence and skill. Are users subjected to an element of "pot luck" when they use a service? (One day they might get an in depth personalised and thorough service from a competent and helpful worker, the next day they could get a curt, unresponsive and ineffective service from a less than competent worker).

• Standards are not targets or vague aspirations. They are a series of minimum guarantees that users should always be able to expect from a service. Quality experts argue that organisations should aim for "zero defects or errors". They suggest that as soon as a margin of error is allowed, the standard will start to slide. Managers need to work with staff to identify standards, train and help staff to ensure that they can be met, publish the standards, check to ensure that they are always met and act quickly if they are not.

Quality affects all aspects of an organisation.

• Staff who have an administrative role, with little direct contact with users are a critical part of a service chain. All staff must be encouraged to see their work in relation to the quality of service provided to the user. For "front line staff" to deliver quality services they must be able to rely on quality management, information, administration and support.

• The role of managers is critical. Quality Assurance needs to be seen as a positive development within an organisation. If staff see it as a management technique designed to "catch them out" then it will probably fail. The development of a quality assurance system should be a participative process that actively involves all staff.

# A model for identifying service quality

Any discussion on quality should take into account the users' perceptions, expectations and experience of using a service. An interesting approach to this was developed by three American academics who studied quality from the point of view of a person using a service rather than that of a person purchasing a product.

Parauraman, Zeithaml and Berry's model can be adapted and developed to look at services from the perspective of someone using a service provided by a voluntary group.

The model has the following attractions:

- It deals with what people "perceive". This is important as quality is often a matter of perception.

- It looks at a service from the point of the user rather than from that of a service provider or funding body.

- Its focus is on specific gaps in expectation and actual experience of using the service.

This model has three distinct advantages:

- It looks at a service from a users point of view – turning the way the service operates inside out.

- It provides staff with a framework to research and establish what exactly are the gaps in how a service is designed and operates.

- Used properly, it recognises that quality is very much a matter of individual perception that will differ from user to user.

# Gaps in service quality

Using the service quality model, a number of gaps can develop, as can be seen in Box 5.3 overleaf.

## Gap 1: between users' expectations and needs and what the service provider thinks the user needs and wants.

People who design and run services usually see the service in a different way from the people who use it. A management committee of a newly established advice centre thought that people would want a service that was friendly and informal. They therefore decided to have an open plan office. It was later established that users would have preferred the privacy of interview rooms.

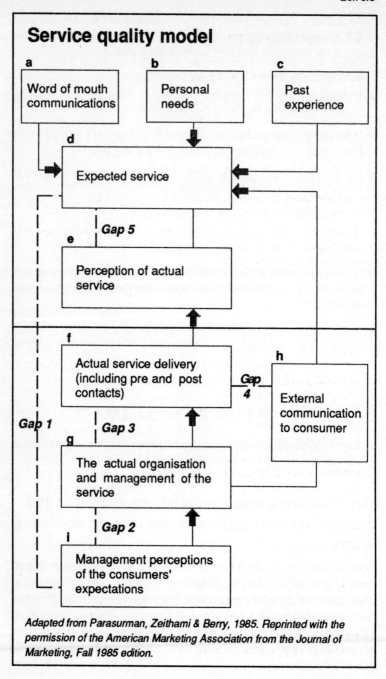

**Service quality model**

a Word of mouth communications

b Personal needs

c Past experience

d Expected service

Gap 5

e Perception of actual service

f Actual service delivery (including pre and post contacts)

Gap 4

h External communication to consumer

Gap 1

Gap 3

g The actual organisation and management of the service

Gap 2

i Management perceptions of the consumers' expectations

Adapted from Parasurman, Zeithami & Berry, 1985. Reprinted with the permission of the American Marketing Association from the Journal of Marketing, Fall 1985 edition.

Box 5.3 continued

# The service quality model explained

Boxes a, b, and c are the factors that influence what each service user expects the service to be like. None of these factors are in the direct control of the service provider. They represent a series of messages, perceptions and actual needs that a person picks up before they use the service. The level and accuracy of this information obviously varies from user to user.

Box h, the external communications produced by the service provider may also influence users. The service provider communicates through publicity material, media and generally by the image of the service.

Boxes a, b, c and h, therefore combine together to create a perception of "expected service" (Box d) This can be a series of positive expectations, or it might be a series of negative ones, or it might be a set of expectations that the service provider regards as unrealistic (. . ."the organisation will be able to solve everything. . .").

Turning to the service provider, the people who design the service and decide how it should be organised have their own views of what users need and want (Box i). This might be accurate and well researched or it could be totally out of touch with users needs and expectations. However, this perception is used along with the level of resources that are available, the policies, history and values of the organisation to design and set up a service  (Box g).

How the service actually works in practice (Box f) is made up of three parts: pre-contact (how the user gains access to the service), the service itself and the post follow up.

Box e  represents what the user actually thinks about the quality and value of the service after using it.

Often the problem is one of not understanding exactly what the need is. A number of large organisations have established that people are dissatisfied with having to wait for appointments. They have responded by improving the physical appearance of the waiting area (eg painting the waiting room, providing newspapers etc) when what people really wanted was to have an accurate appointment time that was kept to.

## Gap 2: between how a service's management would like the service to be managed and how it actually performs.

Gap 2 is a management problem. It reflects an inability to run the organisation in the way that the service managers would like to. The gap may well be caused by inadequate funding or other constraints. For example, an agency would like to have wheelchair access to all parts of its building, but cost and design factors prevent this.

The service management may be unable to bring about the changes in working practice or to recruit and retain staff of sufficient competence and skill to provide the desired level of quality.

## Gap 3: between how a service's management thinks or believes that the service should operate and how it operates in practice.

Just because there are formal quality standards, there is no guarantee that the service will be carried out in the specified way. Individual workers may disagree with or not properly understand, or be unable to work in the way that the organisation thinks that they should.

For example, as part of an agency's quality assurance programme it decided that there should always be three staff available during the centre's public opening hours. However, due to staff absences, other pressures and staff not regarding it as being particularly important on at least two to three occasions in a month sessions were under-staffed. The agency's management did not know this.

## Gap 4: between the day to day reality of the organisation and the image that it creates in its external communications and publicity.

The public image of an organisation may well be very different from how it works in practice. This often creates confused expectations.

A large housing organisation decided that as part of its equal opportunities policy and its commitment to improve the quality of access to translate all of its publicity material into minority ethnic languages. This created an expectation amongst users of such languages that if they were to contact a housing office there would be someone there who could speak to them in their language – this was seldom ever the case.

## Gap 5: between the users expectations of the service and the service they actually receive.

This is the difference between the service that is delivered and what the user had previously expected. It could be that the service is disappointing (. ."I expected that the problem could be sorted out quickly... they tell me now that it will take weeks) or that the quality of service exceeds expectations (..."I did not realise that the service was free. .").

# What is Quality?

Trying to reach a definition of what makes up quality in any particular instance is difficult. However the following elements were found in most cases:

## Information

The availability of information (in different forms) which explains the organisation and the services in a simple way.

Examples:

- Producing a user guide in a "plain English style".
- "It is now standard practice to explain every step of the process to the groups we are working with and to refer them to where they can get background information"
                              – *a community development project*

## Reliability

The knowledge that a service will be carried out as agreed and to an agreed time.

Examples:

- Agreeing a personal contract with long term users – and keeping to it.

- "We now give people a definite time for home visits – we record the times we are late or miss the appointment."

## Competence and accuracy

The staff have the required degree of skill and knowledge to provide a service competently.

Examples:

- A social work agency ensures that one in five advice casework files are checked to see that the right advice was given and that all calculations were correct.

- "We are making plans to use the National Vocational Qualifications scheme to ensure that all staff are trained and qualified" *– a welfare rights organisation*

## Effective access

The first point of contact with the organisation encourages the person to use the service, and the service feels "approachable". Also there is a an equality of access amongst users.

- A programme of initiatives to find out how people with disabilities could use the service better.

- "We have made special efforts so that peole with children feel comfortable coming to our classes." *a health promotion project*

## Effective redress

When things go wrong or when a user feels that they have had poor service or unfair treatment they are able to quickly have things put right.

- The development of complaints procedures, advocacy and published users rights.

Box 5.4

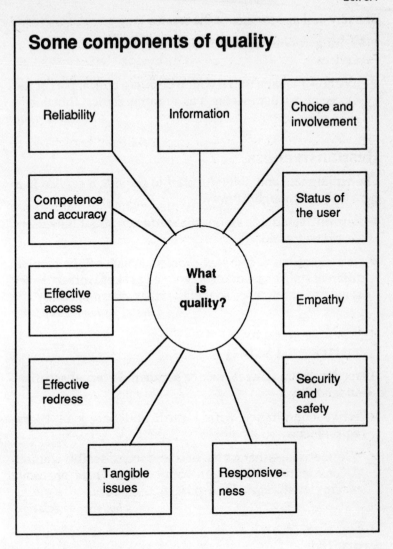

# Some components of quality

- Reliability
- Information
- Choice and involvement
- Competence and accuracy
- Status of the user
- Effective access
- **What is quality?**
- Empathy
- Effective redress
- Security and safety
- Tangible issues
- Responsive-ness

● "Staff have been trained so that if anyone makes a fair complaint, formal or informal, they are responsible for putting things right and not just defending or apportioning blame." — *a residential home*

# Tangible issues

The physical appearance of the service.

- Waiting rooms, public image, telephone and reception services.

- "We now manage the reception desk as a critical part of the service rather than seeing it as a routine clerical function."

*– a health clinic*

# Responsiveness

The willingness and ability of staff to provide a service in a personal and thoughtful way.

- Agreeing standards amongst a staff team about how users should be treated.

- "If a client has a complex problem which might involve different staff, one worker is assigned as "key worker" to act as a point of reference so that the client doesn't get lost".

*– a hostel for homeless people*

# Security and safety

A freedom from danger, risk or accident. Personal security. Confidentiality.

- Active compliance with Health and Safety at Work requirements.

- "We now realise that we have access to considerable amount of confidential information about users. There are now systems for storage and disposal of users files."

*– a housing association*

# Empathy

The degree to which staff listen to and explain things to individual users.

- Encouragement and support to staff to work with a client to design personal services which meet an individual needs at the same time as meeting the organisations standards and practices.

- "We now spend more time with users working out what it is they exactly want". *– an employment centre*

## Choice and involvement

The ability of a user to influence the type and level of service provided.

- The amount of consultation, involvement in decisions (and the support to participate fully) available to the user.

- "We regard it as standard practice that clients should be fully informed of all options open to them and have them fully explained."

## Status of the user

The degree of respect given to the client. What does it feel like to be a user?

- Managing a service in such a way that see users as people with needs and rights rather than "people with problems".

- "Staff are now trained to explain everything to clients."
*– a health clinic*

# Developing Quality Standards

An important part of a quality approach to management is the drawing up of a number of key standards that someone using a service should always be able to expect. A critical part of the quality assurance process is that of checking to ensure that the agreed standards are always being met.

A standard can be defined as something which is:

- Agreed and understood by all staff.

- Objective and unambiguous.

- A commitment that people using the service should always be able to expect.

- A minimum level of competence or efficiency which should always be present.

- So clearly defined that it should be obvious to all concerned if the standard is not being met.

- Capable of being consistently met. The organisation believes that it has staffing levels, budgets and other resources capable of meeting the standard.

Drawing up service standards is about identifying a threshold or minimum level that a service must always be able to achieve. They should not be confused with longer term objectives or targets.

There are some clear advantages in developing standards within an organisation:

They can create a "clarity of purpose" within an organisation. Often staff are not sure of what is expected of them (job descriptions are vague, management does not give adequate supervision and training..). Active discussion about standards and regular monitoring of them can overcome a lack of consistency within an organisation (everyone doing the job as they think best. . . ) and create better self monitoring.

The adoption of standards can help the organisation to identify staff training and development needs. Standards can be related to training based competencies (something which the development of National Vocational Qualifications, NVQs, is likely to make more important).

Standards can form the basis of encouraging users or clients to enhance their status within the organisation. They can easily be described and publicised as "rights" that users have.

Developing standards can be a creative process of establishing what are the important values that should guide the organisation's work. Standards should be a practical statement of what the organisation sees as being important.

Box 5.5

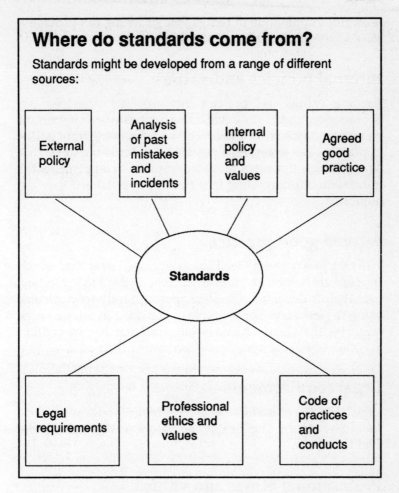

# Where do standards come from?

Standards might be developed from a range of different sources:

- External policy
- Analysis of past mistakes and incidents
- Internal policy and values
- Agreed good practice

**Standards**

- Legal requirements
- Professional ethics and values
- Code of practices and conducts

# Where standards come from

## External policy

A funding body might have expectations and policies that organisations that it funds or enters into contracts with must meet. These expectations need to be clarified as they are often implicit or "assumed".

# Analysis of past mistakes and incidents

A careful examination of things that go wrong can provide a constructive basis for future standards

# Internal policies and values

Turning values and policies into working practices. An organisation might want equal opportunities to be an important value. Standards are one practical way of moving from policy to practice. For example, a possible standards might be that "the centre will always make appropriate arrangements for translation or interpreting facilities to be available if they are requested."

# Agreed good practice

Working practices may well have developed over time which staff feel are helpful and useful. Publishing them as a standard could help to develop a consistent approach and be of particular value to new staff. For example, a standard in advice work might be "that clients should be informed that they are entitled to copies of all correspondence concerning their case".

# Legal requirements

Legislation imposes a number of requirements on how a service should be run eg. The Health and Safety At Work Act or the Childrens Act.

# Professional ethics and values

Staff may be required to conform to practices and rules of the professional body of which they are a member, for example, solicitors and the Law Society's regulations.

# Codes of practice and conduct

The organisation may subscribe to codes of "good practice" published by a national agency, and which might provide the basis of some standards.

# The value of standards

There is a danger of compiling standards that are only of superficial importance. It is easier to identify standards about choice in the canteen than about the degree of choice for clients in the core service they receive.

Standards are only valuable if they relate to the elements of the service that the users think important. The objective should be to have a range of quality standards that are comprehensive enough to cover the important elements of the service, rather than trying to "standardise" every single aspect of an organisation's work.

In putting the standards together, it is necessary to be thorough and ensure that the standards that are agreed are ones that the organisation is capable of meeting with the levels of available staffing and budgets. Standards are *minimum* levels of service that should consistently be met.

An exercise that can develop out of agreeing minimum standards is to identify *"standards plus"* – levels of service which the organisation would like to be able to meet i.e. that are above the threshold of the standard, but can not always guarantee. For example, an information service might have a quality standard of responding to every enquiry within three working days. If it is able to meet this standard, it could then go onto commit itself to a "standard plus" policy of a two day response time and a three month follow up telephone call to every fifth user to check on the effectiveness of the information provided. It could then monitor itself to see how many times it exceeds the standard. This could indicate that the original standard is too low, or that the staff have reached an excellent level of competence.

Box 5.6

# Using standards positively – a case study

The housing charity Shelter has a network of housing aid centres providing free, confidential, impartial information and practical help on housing rights and opportunities throughout the country.

In April 1991 after 18 months of extensive staff consultation and participation it published, for internal use, a document entitled "Shelter Housing Aid: Casework Standards."

The document is intended to be a working document for Shelter's staff setting out common standards and practices based upon practical experience of what works well.

Areas covered in the document include record systems, procedures for dealing with difficult cases or for running team meetings. Each section has the following:

- A statement setting out an expectation i.e. what each worker should be able to do.
- Some background information explaining the thoughts behind the expectation.
- Some examples of how the expectation might be implemented.
- A guide to possible methods to be used.
- Some practical advice on how to attain the standard through appropriate training, team support and written materials.

The style of the document is helpful and supportive rather than prescriptive or directive.

Shelter sees that the approach has three main benefits:

It provides a framework for staff training and development, particularly for new staff.

It brings a diverse and sometimes isolated network together, creates some consistency across the organisation and helps managers and staff to see what is expected of them.

It helps staff in busy centres to make priorities and have an "overview" of their work.

# A formal registration for a quality standard – BS5750/IS9000

In 1979 the British Standards Institute (BSI) launched BS5750. It sets out the steps and processes suppliers and manufacturers must take in order to be awarded BS5750. It does not prescribe specific standards for an individual product or service, rather it tests the system that produces the product or service.

BSI claim that BS5750 is suitable for all kinds of industries and organisations of whatever size producing any kind of product or service. By 1991, over 11,000 firms (including a an increasing number of public bodies) had obtained BS5750. It has been adopted as an international standard known as the ISO 9000 series. The European equivalent is called EN 29000.

Registering for BS5750 has the following advantages:

It is a statement that the organisation has systems and procedures aimed at producing a quality product or service which have been independently inspected and are subject to regular audit.

By referring to BS5750 accreditation it might assist in establishing external credibility in order to win contracts.

The process of obtaining BS5750 may well improve the organisation's internal processes and management. an important argument in quality assurance is "get it right first time" on the basis that doing things properly in the first instance is always cheaper and quicker than making errors and having to put them right later.

To register for BS5750 an organisation is required to produce detailed systems, usually in the form of a quality manual, which is reviewed by an external assessor (there are about ten firms who do this, including BSI itself).

The organisation must be able to demonstrate that it has systems and management procedures in place that ensure quality. The following elements are usually included:

• Quality Assurance Policy.

- Training programmes for all staff in quality assurance.

- Clear staff responsibilities for quality.

- Inspection, monitoring and testing systems.

- Quality control (i.e. checking the output).

- Systems that will quickly identify error and enable remedial or corrective action.

- Records and statistical systems to monitor quality and provide good management information.

- Clear organisational procedures for staff.

- Effective purchasing policies.

- Systems that can effectively "trace" a piece of work through an organisation and check on different stages.

- An audit process for quality.

BS5750 does not say what are the quality elements of any service or product. It is only concerned with the process and systems involved in planning for, managing and controlling quality. There is some debate about the ease of application of BS5750 to a "people" sector such as social care. BSI do suggest that it can be adapted to any type of organisation, but there is very little evidence of any real take up within the voluntary sector. The total cost of registration varies, but, for small organisations £3,000 would be a reasonable estimate, annual certificates and further external inspections would be around £1,500. The staff time involved in preparing for assessment is considerable and would need to be budgeted for. There is also a danger of too many systems, procedures and manuals creating an organisation ran by a rulebook which de-motivates staff and reduces the flexibility of service and its responsiveness to changing needs.

At this stage, it is difficult to arrive at a definitive position on the relevance of BS5750 to voluntary organisations. If contracts for care continue  to develop at a pace, and the awarding of contracts becomes more competitive then there may be some value, perhaps only for large organisations, in considering BS5750 further.

# Summary

1. How do you find out about what your users regard as "quality"?

2. Do you think about the different perceptions that your users might have? A 16-year old will probably want different things from a service (or for it to be delivered in a different way) than a senior citizen.

3. How do you avoid quality assurance becoming an inflexible paper generating exercise?

4. What standards do you currently have? How are they recorded?

5. How will you use quality assurance as a developmental tool, in staff training, supervision and support?

# Hill Street Community Centre
## >> the continuing story

Six months later the council published its draft proposals for service agreements between it and voluntary agencies. A key part of it was on measuring the quality of service. Voluntary agencies were to put forward proposals for how they intended to ensure the quality and effective performance of the services that they intended to run.

At Hill Street Community Centre, Hilary the co-ordinator was now very experienced at dealing with what seemed like a constant stream of new initiatives from the council. "Quality" was an interesting idea. It clearly went a lot further than simply counting how many people were using the centre in order to fill in a performance review form.

Hilary proposed that the centre's management committee should organise a special meeting to look at the issue and come up with some sort of statement of quality.

At the special meeting they worked through a number of questions:

- What criteria does each individual use to judge the centre's work?

- What is good work? How do we know when things are working well?

- What would be the worst community centre? How would it work? What would it be like?

- How do we know what local people want? What does it feel like to use the centre?

The discussion was a useful one. It emerged that everyone had some sort of expectation or criteria by which they informally evaluated the centre and, perhaps, most importantly, they had very little real knowledge of what individuals who lived in the area thought about or wanted from the centre.

The committee agreed to work on these issues and to try to come up with some quality standards (or guarantee of what to expect) by which the centre could be measured by funders, users and themselves. They would also us a limited number of performance indicators to provide "base line" monitoring information such as opening hours and usage. It would be a difficult and time consuming task, however, they felt that it could be a worthwhile one.

However when Hilary, sticking to her example, wondered just what criteria could be applied to the two minibuses, the meeting was more or less stumped. You could measure the costs of the service, but surely what mattered was its quality.

Looking back, Hilary recognised that the centre was now in a position to be much more clear about how its work should be measured. There was less danger of being bounced into agreeing to a measurement system that gave a distorted picture of what the centre was about.

# CHAPTER 6
# MANAGING THE NEW RELATIONSHIP

The development of a "contract culture" for social care fundamentally changes the relationship between statutory authorities, voluntary organisations and service users.

The new relationship is often displayed as a triangular one:

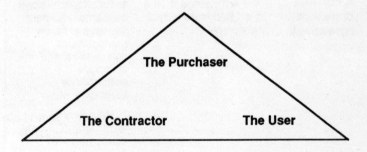

The purchaser is the local authority or health authority that provides the funding for the contract and sets out what is to be done (often called the specification). The voluntary organisation that enters into a contract to provide the service is called the "contractor" and the term "user" represents whoever it is intended will benefit from the service provided.

Box 6.1

# The different funding relationships

This table sets out how the relationship between funders and voluntary organisations seems to be changing

| FUNDING SYSTEM | ATTITUDE OF FUNDER | RELATIONSHIP |
|---|---|---|
| Open ended grants | "If we still like you next year, we will probably give you money again". | Vague relationship. Grants officer or councillors sit on management committee. Occasional liaison visits to keep in touch. |
| Grants with conditions | "We will give you a grant subject to you agreeing to some conditions (eg You will have an equal opportunities policy and maintain records)." | As above, but slightly more focused on specific conditions and outputs. |
| A contract or service agreement | "We will change from a grant to a more formal agreement." | 1. Relationship stays the same – funders continue to sit on management committees, and now also have performance measures, etc *or*.<br><br>2. Relationship is at "arms length" – only concerned with measuring performance against agreed objectives. |
| Tightly defined contract | "We are in this contract to achieve a defined level of service from an independent organisation at an agreed price. | A client/contractor relationship. Both parties have clear duties and rights. |

# Managing a new relationship

'Most of the attention so far has centred on the relationship between the purchaser and the contractor. It is a very clear relationship as it involves a formal negotiation and contracting process. The relationship that the user has with either the purchaser or the contractor has received much less attention.

A contract for services (or service agreement) assumes a defined and more structured relationship than one based on grant aid. However, in practice, some councillors and officers want to keep the informal relationships and the involvement in the organisation's management process to which they are accustomed.

In moving from a grant to a contract a voluntary organisation needs to identify how the relationship can best develop and how the funding body (or contract purchasers) legitimate need for performance and monitoring information can best be managed.

Box 6.2

## Some possible relationships

This table suggests some possible relationships that can be developed:

| level of contact | unspecified ← arrangement → specified |  |
|---|---|---|
| high | Active involvement in the management process | Partnership: Regular liaison as well as a formal measurement process. |
| low | Occasional contact through periodic reviews and visits | Arms length formal contract management |

79

# Occasional contact through periodic reviews and visits

The relationship between the voluntary organisation and the funder is not a particularly structured one. It might include the annual production of statistics and a report of work, the authority might have the ability to attend management committee meetings or carry out infrequent evaluation exercises or monitoring visits. The only real monitoring takes place when the funding arrangement or contract is up for renewal. The funder in such cases, working on the basis of "out of sight – out of mind", may find it easier to make cuts.

This type of relationship gives the voluntary group considerable independence to get on with its work as it sees best. However, there is a danger that, because of a lack of communication, the funding body fails to understand or appreciates the groups work and may well carry out a monitoring exercise or make decisions based on ignorance.

# Active involvement in the management process

The funding body is significantly involved in the operational management of the voluntary group. It will take a full part in the management process through formal channels (eg through being very involved in the recruitment and selection of staff) and through regular consultation and full access to management information. This can either be done in a co-operative (or cosy) way or through the funder exercising (or threatening to exercise) a veto.

It could be argued that the voluntary organisation is really only acting as the "agent" of the funder – carrying out their policies and meeting their objectives. The closeness of the relationship can cause some difficulties. For example in negotiating future grants or contracts, the funder would probably have full access to detailed costings which could give them an unfair advantage.

Sometimes, problems may occur because the relationship is too unstructured and too informal.

## Partnership – regular liaison as well as a formal measurement process

There is some recognition that the voluntary body is an independent organisation with its own aims and objectives. Representatives of the funding body are in close contact with the organisation, through liaison visits and regular joint meetings.

The relationship is one of providing advice, consultation and planning. It is important that the respective roles are clarified and recorded. There is a potential for the funding body to have "two bites at the cake" – through informal contact (eg attending management committees) and through a formal contract or performance measurement system.

## Arms length formal contract management

The relationship that the statutory authority has with the voluntary organisation is the same as it has with all of its other service suppliers (eg British Telecom). It has formal specifications for the quantity and quality of the service to be provided and at what cost.

The contract (either through its original specification or in an appendix to it) will clearly state the respective responsibilities of the funder and the voluntary organisation. The contract management process is a structured one between two clearly independent parties.

The relationship is formal and distant. How the voluntary agency manages itself is of little concern to the funder provided it gives the service that it said that it would.

# Reviewing the relationship

In reviewing these relationships a number of points are worth considering:

# Consistency

In the move from grant aid to a more clearly defined contractual relationship it is important to discuss openly what sort of relationships there needs to be between the parties involved.

One voluntary agency reported negotiating an agreement for providing a service rather than applying for grant. Although there were definite advantages in having a service agreement, it involved the agency in many more management tasks and because of the more explicit nature of the agreement led to a more formal monitoring process by council officers.

The agency's co-ordinator described the new relationship as "the worst of both worlds" in that at one level the council wanted a new, more independent, contractual relationship and at another, councillors wanted to continue to attend the agency's management committee, and be fully involved in the management process (including discussions on the negotiating strategy for future meetings with council officers on the funding agreement). In effect, the council had both a formal "arms length agreement" and full participation in the agency's management process at the same time.

# Disparity between different funders

A voluntary group that receives funding or has contracts with more than one source will have to establish a different type of relationship with each funder. Producing different information for different needs, responding to each separate monitoring process and conducting different sets of information will all have implications for staff time and cost. Experience in the USA indicates that this has become a huge problem for many small to medium sized groups dependant on state contracts.

# The relationship changes over time

It is useful to see the relationship as a dynamic one which changes over time. If a group has too close a relationship to its funders than its independence and ability to properly manage itself may suffer. Alternatively, a relationship which is too

Box 6.3

# Types of monitoring reports

A voluntary organisation needs to decide how best it should report to its funding body. Three reporting systems are possible:

## Achievement and progress reports

The voluntary organisation sends in reports as and when it has something significant to report or has completed an important aspect of its work programme.

## By exception reports

When something goes wrong or when an agreed standard is not being met, the obligation is on the voluntary organisation to report on it. For example, a community transport service might have to report each time it has to cancel a service.

## Regular reports

A report every month or every quarter with fixed information.

---

formal and structured may be inflexible and make negotiating change difficult.

Often change in the relationship is caused by a change in personnel- different people (either on the funders or on the voluntary groups side) may have different perceptions and background knowledge. Or it could be that when adequate funds are available and there is support for the groups work the relationship is more likely to be a close one and when funds are short it is more likely to become distant.

# Monitoring and inspection

Changes in the organisation of community care, greater public concern about the standards of care (particularly in residential care) and development of "partnership" relations between public and voluntary sectors have all led to the strengthening of monitoring and inspection arrangements.

Monitoring can be defined as the process of collecting information, data and results as a way of providing some assurance that a service is being managed to agreed standards.

Inspection, in the context of community care, is defined by the Social Services Inspectorate in their guidance notes, "Inspecting for Quality", as "the evaluation of a service or set of services at a particular point in time, including:

- the resources devoted to the provision of the service;
- the processes involved in providing the service;
- the quality and quantity of service provision;
- the quality of life of the users."

The Inspectorate's guidance stress "that evaluation should be carried out against previously agreed aims and objectives, including standards." It also points out that inspections can be planned or be announced or unannounced.

A voluntary organisation should not feel threatened by inspection or monitoring visits. Being open to fair judgement and criticism is reasonable. However, for the process to work in the interest of all parties there needs to be some agreement in advance between the staff carrying out the monitoring visit or inspection and the voluntary organisation, covering the following points:

# The principles

What is the purpose of the monitoring exercise? Who do the staff carrying out the monitoring exercise report to?

Are there published terms of reference for the monitoring exercise? If so, how do they relate to the aims and objectives of the organisation?

How will the monitoring exercise take into account the level of resources available to the organisation to run the service? There is little point in a monitoring exercise assessing the level and

Box 6.4

# Inspecting for quality

The Social Services Inspectorate's guidance notes, "Inspecting for Quality", suggests some useful principles for local authorities in developing an inspection function for the implementation of Community Care policies:

- **Explicit and measurable**
The Inspections process should be: **Rooted in explicit values and measurable standards.**

The inspection should be based upon clear statements of intent – service plans, standards, good practice notes, etc.

- **Anti discriminatory**
Inspections should take into account race, culture, religion, gender, age and disability issues when reviewing the accessibility and availability of services. Staff within inspection units should reflect the equality of opportunity, anti-discriminatory and anti racist strategies.

- **Publicly visible**
The activities of the inspection unit should be publicly known and accountable through the authority's committee system.

- **Impartial and Equitable**
All parties should feel that the inspection is carried out in a fair manner which creates confidence.

- **Consistent**
The methods used by the inspection unit should be consistent over time and across services.

- **Reliable and unprejudiced**
The inspection process should aim to gather objective evidence which can be independently validated.

- **Flexible**
The inspection process should be capable of responding to unforeseen demands.

- **Protection to the user**
The existence of an inspection unit should give protection to a service user by inspecting services regularly, sometimes unannounced and when emergencies arise.

*Reprinted with the permission of HMSO.*

Box 6.5

# A monitoring code of conduct

The Housing Corporation is responsible for monitoring the performance of Housing Associations. It has published a Monitoring Code of Conduct which sets out how it expects its monitoring staff to carry out their work.

It sets out the following issues:

• Impartiality
That monitors will have high professional standards and will eliminate personal views, interests or prejudice.

That monitors should declare any personal interest in an association and also that monitors should avoid becoming involved in any staff employment matters within an association.

• Consistency
That monitors are responsible for keeping up to date with standards and to make and be able to justify any judgements against such standards.

• Confidentiality
That monitors should treat information obtained in the course of monitoring as confidential and if a list of pre-visit information is requested, that a timetable for the exercise and issuing of reports is produced.

quality of a service without first assessing the level of resources available.

What criteria will be used to judge the information gathered by the monitoring exercise? How clear are the criteria and how do they relate to the organisations values and purpose?

## The process

Is it appropriate that there should be unannounced monitoring visits? If so how should they be carried out?

What information will be needed by the monitoring staff? Is there any information – client records, staff records or details of arrangements with other funders that should be regarded as confidential and either not be released or only released with specific conditions?

How much time will be given over to the monitoring exercise? What will the timetable be for producing a final report?

Will the voluntary organisation be able to comment on a draft of any monitoring report?

What specialist knowledge will monitoring officers have?

What is the brief given to the monitoring officers? Do they operate to any code of practice or systematic approach?

## Monitoring and the users

How will users be able to contribute to the monitoring process?

How will users have independent access to the monitoring officers?

## The results of the monitoring

There are a number of important points to consider when deciding what to do with the results of the monitoring. Who will have access to any monitoring report? Will it be a public document?

If the voluntary organisation believes that there are factual errors or that the report contains unfair judgements, how will it be able to communicate such beliefs?

If the report is critical, how will the voluntary organisation take this in a positive light as an opportunity to develop and enhance the service, alter it or simply defend the status quo? If there is a need for change, how will this process of change be taken forward?

# Chapter 7
# MANAGEMENT IMPLICATIONS

Developing systems for performance measurement or quality assurance has the potential to considerably change the internal management processes within an organisation and change how managers work and see their role.

The following eight issues need to be addressed:

## 1. Watching the scoreboard and not the game

The introduction of a performance measurement system and the attention paid to it could mean that managers focus their attention on getting a "good result on the indicator" and ignore the informal aspects of the service (atmosphere, staff client relations) which the indicators are unlikely to report on.

## 2. Too many systems

There is a tendency that when an organisation starts drawing up procedures, systems and monitoring processes it is unable to stop itself. Careful management is needed to prevent quality assurance and performance measurement systems degenerating into a time and paper consuming exercise that pull staff away from delivering a service and thus reduces performance.

Some control needs to be exercised to ensure that the focus is on the "quality" of the information to be collected, rather than the quantity of it.

## 3. Standards and inflexibility

Performance standards must take into account flexibility and responsiveness to the specific needs of individuals and not used to produce a rigid service which fails to respond to needs. Flexibility and responsiveness need to be written into standards.

## 4. What gets measured gets done

Staff could take into account what is being measured and use it as a guide (in the absence of anything else) as to where they should direct their efforts. This would be acceptable if the range of indicators being used give a full picture of all of the issues and priorities involved. However, if they do not, then it could cause problems for both staff and managers.

A further issue is whether an organisation's performance can be directly related to an individual's performance. If performance indicators are such that they can be directly related to an individual member of staff then it is logical that they should be used in supervision and staff appraisal. However, before doing so it is important to determine to what extent did the individual member of staff have direct control over performance – it could be that the actual performance was caused by external circumstances that s/he could not affect however hard s/he worked.

## 5. What about the things that we cannot measure?

Performance measures, by their very nature, involve the elements in an organisation that can in some way be counted and recorded. However, there may be things that an organisation regards as important, but, does not develop measures for. There are three reasons for doing this:

The time or cost involved in measurement is judged to be excessive.

The process of measurement is regarded as unacceptable by users eg. it disrupts the service or is perceived as a threat to confidentiality.

The issue involved is particularly difficult to measure in any reliable way (eg, the atmosphere and quality of relationships between staff and users).

The difficulties of determining effective measures can be exaggerated. However, as the Audit Commission said, "the art in performance monitoring lies in ensuring that the measurable does not drive out the immeasurable".

Managers would be foolish to ignore things like teamwork, humour, working styles and informal reactions from users. Review sessions, evaluation workshops, independent appraisals and user meetings may all be needed to give a flavour to the data and information generated through formal measurement.

## 6. As objectives change so must methods of measurement

Voluntary organisations are rarely static. As they respond to new needs or move into new areas of work it is important to check that the performance measurement systems used or the perception about user quality are still valid and would report accurately.

In developing work plans and work programmes, it is useful to identify specific indicators that can be used to monitor progress towards each objective. If it is not possible to identify indicators for an objective it probably means that the objective is far too vague and open ended.

## 7. Having to run two systems

In an ideal world a funding body and a voluntary organisation would be able to agree systems which satisfy the funders need to know that their money is being used properly and the voluntary organisation's need to know that it works in a way that meets its aims, policies and values.

There are occasions where this ideal state can be reached. However, there are occasions when a funder insists on using indicators which often fail to report anything of value or when the funder is not interested in establishing useful measures or does not share the same values and policies as the voluntary organisation.

If a voluntary organisation agrees to use measures that it feels are inappropriate then there is a danger of the measures distorting the internal management process and after a time (in the absence of any other information) setting the direction for the organisation. It may well be that an organisation has to run a performance measurement system to provide "inappropriate" information to a funder and at the same time develop its own internal systems to measure and evaluate the factors that it regards as important.

## 8. External measurement can reduce performance

A local authority decided to require the voluntary groups that it funded to produce performance measures. The management committee of an education project were anxious that if the project failed to produce good evidence of its performance it could face reductions in its funding. A key indicator was the number of "outreach" sessions that the project would run in local community centres. The project co-ordinator knew that on average they were able to run twenty two sessions per month, however, to be "on the safe side", he committed the project to a target of eighteen sessions per month and filled in quarterly performance reviews.

In the first year the project easily met its commitment of eighteen and in fact regularly passed it by running over twenty sessions. In subsequent years, the project only ever ran a maximum of eighteen sessions per month. New staff would question the value of doing more than eighteen sessions. After all, that was all that the performance measure required.

# BIBLIOGRAPHY

## Contracts for Care

### Getting Ready For Contracts
by Sandy Adirondack and Richard Macfarlane. Directory of Social Change, Radius Works, Back Lane, London NW3 1HL
*Comprehensive guide for voluntary organisations on moving from grant aid to contracts.*

### Purchase of Service
Social Services Inspectorate, HMSO. 1991.
*A practice guide to contracting and quality.*

### Inspecting for Quality
Social Services Inspectorate, HMSO. 1991.
*Guidance to local authorities on the operation of inspection units.*

### Evaluation for Voluntary Organisations
"Evaluation in the Voluntary Sector" by Mog Ball. Forbes Trust, 1988. Available from Directory of Social Change, Radius Works, Back Lane, London NW3 1HL.
*Useful guide to evaluation.*

## Working Effectively

By Warren Feek, Bedford Square Press. 1988. Available from 26 Bedford Square, London WC1B 3HU.
*Step by step approach to self evaluation.*

## Questions of Value

The Law Centres Federation. 1988. Available from Duchess House, 18 Warren Street, London, W1P 5DB.
*A five part Introduction to evaluation for Law Centres.*

## Performance Measurement

Performance Measurement - getting the concepts right
Public Finance Foundation. 1988. Available from 3 Robert Street, London, WC2N 6BH.
*Mainly aimed at public sector organisations, a useful guide to core concepts.*

## Measuring Quality: The Patient's View Of Day Surgery

The Audit Commission. May 1991. Available from 1 Vincent Square, London SW1 2PN
*Includes an interesting draft questionnaire to guage patient reaction.*

# Value for Money

## Getting Value For Money

CIPFA. 1987. Available from 3 Robert Street, London, WC2N 6BH.
*The accompanying guide to a video based training pack.*

## Value For Money Auditing

Price Waterhouse. 1990. Available from Gee & Co, South Quay Plaza, 183 Marsh Wall, London E14 9FS.
*Detailed guide to Local Authority staff on carrying out value for money reviews.*

# Quality

### The Search for Quality
John Stewart and Kieron Walsh. 1989. Available from Local Government Management Board Arndale House, Arndale Centre, Luton, LU1 2TS.
*Aimed at local authorities, a thoughtful introduction on quality in service organisations.*

### Quality and Contracts
Association of Metropolitan Authorities. 1991. Available from 35 Great Smith Street, London, SW1P 3BJ.
*Case material and practice notes on developing quality assurance.*

### DTI publications
The Department of Trade and Industry publishes a number of free booklet on quality management. Although aimed at manufacturing industries, they provide useful background reading. The publications list is available from the DTI, c/o Mediascene, PO Box 20, Hengoed, Mid Glamorgan, CF8 9EP. Tel 0443 821877.

### BS 5750
Information regarding BS5750 can be obtained from BSI Quality Assurance, PO Box 375, Milton Keynes, MK14 6LL.

### Guidance document on BS5750 in Social Care Agencies
The British Quality Association. Available from 10 Grosvenor Gardens, London SW1W 0DQ.